NEW AMERICANS

Mexican Americans

by Jayne Keedle

Series Consultant: Judith A. Warner, Ph.D.,
Professor of Sociology and Criminal Justice,
Texas A&M International University

Marshall Cavendish
Benchmark
New York

Marshall Cavendish Benchmark
99 White Plains Road
Tarrytown, NY 10591
www.marshallcavendish.us

All Internet addresses were correct and accurate at the time of printing.

Library of Congress Cataloging-in-Publication Data

Keedle, Jayne.
Mexican Americans / by Jayne Keedle.
p. cm. — (New Americans)
Includes bibliographical references and index.
ISBN 978-0-7614-4307-0
1. Mexican Americans—History—Juvenile literature. 2. Mexican Americans—Juvenile literature. I. Title.
E184.M5K428 2010
973'.046872—dc22 2008052101

Developed for Marshall Cavendish Benchmark by RJF Publishing LLC
Robert Famighetti, President
www.RJFpublishing.com
Design: Westgraphix LLC/Tammy West
Photo Research: Edward A. Thomas
Map Illustrator: Stefan Chabluk
Index: Nila Glikin

Photo credits: Cover, 5, 27, 29, 35, 38, 42, 45, 51, 53, 60, 63, 64, 66, 68, 71: AP/Wide World Photos; 1, 8, 12: Alamy; 6: © Jan Butchofsky-Houser/CORBIS; 16: Library of Congress LC-USZC4-2957; 21: National Archives; 22: Library of Congress LC-DIG-fsa-8b31661; 30: Getty Images; 32: REUTERS/Lucy Nicholson /Landov; 36: © Jim West/Alamy; 48: Robert E Daemmrich/Getty Images; 54: © Ann Johansson/Corbis; 57: © North Wind Picture Archives/ Alamy; 58: AFP/Getty Images; 61: Columbia Pictures Corporation/Photofest.

Cover: Dancers perform at a Cinco de Mayo celebration in the historic Olvera Street district of Los Angeles.

Printed in Malaysia.

135642

CONTENTS

Words defined in the glossary are in **bold** type the first time they appear in the text.

INTRODUCTION

The United States has embraced immigration for most of its history—and has been a destination of choice for people seeking a better life. Today hundreds of thousands of immigrants arrive each year to live and work and make their way in a new country. These "New Americans" come for many reasons, and they come from places all over the world. They bring with them new customs, languages, and traditions—and face many challenges in their adopted country. Over time, they and their children are changed by and become part of the American mainstream culture. At the same time, the mainstream is itself changed as it absorbs many elements of the immigrants' cultures, from ethnic foods to ideas from non-Western belief systems. An understanding of the New Americans, and how they will form part of the American future, is essential for everyone.

This series focuses on recent immigrants from eight major countries and regions: the Caribbean and Central America, China, India and other South Asian countries, Korea, Mexico, Russia and Eastern Europe, Southeast Asia, and West Africa.

Each of these geographic areas is a major source of the millions of immigrants who have come to the United States in the last decades of the twentieth century and the beginning of the twenty-first. For many of these people, the opportunity to move to the United States was opened up by the major

New Americans being sworn in as U.S. citizens.

changes in U.S. immigration law that occurred in the 1960s. For others, the opportunity or imperative to immigrate was triggered by events in their own countries, such as the collapse of Communism in Eastern Europe or civil wars in Central America.

Some of the New Americans found sizable communities of Americans from the same ethnic background and had the benefit of "ethnic neighborhoods" to move into where they could feel welcome and get help adjusting to American life. Many of these communities originated in a previous major wave of immigration, from the 1880s to 1920. Some of the New Americans found very few predecessors to ease the transition as they faced the challenges of adjustment.

These volumes tell the stories of the New Americans, including the personal accounts of a number of immigrants and their children who agreed to be interviewed by some of the authors. As you read, you will learn about the countries of origin and the cultures of these newcomers to American society. You will learn, as well, about how the New Americans are enriching, as they adapt to, American life.

Judith A. Warner, Ph.D.
Professor of Sociology and Criminal Justice
Texas A&M International University

Olvera Street in Los Angeles celebrates the city's Mexican heritage.

CHAPTER ONE

The Mexican-American Community Today

The smell of tacos and the sound of mariachi music waft from outdoor cafes onto Olvera Street. This famous street is part of the city of Los Angeles's El Pueblo de Los Angeles Historical Monument district. The historic district celebrates, among other things, Los Angeles's **Hispanic** heritage, dating back to the founding of the California city in 1781 by Spanish **missionaries** who had traveled north from present-day Mexico. The historic district is dominated by a Mexican–style plaza, a central square that springs to life with folk dancing, strolling guitar players, and festivals celebrating Mexican **culture**—all reminders of the city's early settlers.

Mexican Americans have a long history in the United States—and not just in Los Angeles. In fact, until the mid-1800s, the present-day states of Texas, California, Arizona,

Spectators enjoy a Mexican Independence Day parade in Chicago's Little Village neighborhood.

New Mexico, Nevada, and Utah, as well as parts of Colorado and Wyoming, were all part of Mexico. By **annexation**, war, treaties, and purchases between 1845 and 1853, the region became part of the United States. From this time, there has been a large Mexican-American population in the Southwest, and there are now long-established Mexican-American communities in that region.

In the early twentieth century, many Mexicans came to the United States to escape the violence and uncertainty of the Mexican Revolution (1910–1920). Since then, many more have come in search of work and better lives for themselves and their children.

By the Numbers

According to U.S. Bureau of the Census estimates, in 2006 more than 28.3 million people of Mexican origin were living in the United States. Almost one of every ten Americans is Mexican American, and Mexican Americans account for almost two-thirds of the total U.S. Hispanic population. Though many Mexican Americans have deep roots in what is now the United States, others are recent transplants.

The number of Mexican **immigrants** rose dramatically in the 1990s. The booming U.S. **economy** and economic crises in Mexico brought many people across the border in search of jobs and to join family members already in the United States. In 2006, the Census Bureau estimated there were nearly 11.4 million foreign-born Mexican Americans living in the United States. Almost two-thirds of them had entered the country since 1990.

Also in 2006 about 14 percent of all **documented** immigrants coming to the United States came from Mexico, more than from any other country. The number of documented Mexican immigrants that year was more than 170,000 people. A documented immigrant is one who has a **visa**, issued by the U.S. government, allowing that person to enter the country and live in the United States permanently.

Documented **immigration** tells only part of the story of recent immigration from Mexico. According to one U.S. government report, in the late 1990s and the first five years of the twenty-first century, several hundred thousand people a year entered the United States from Mexico without documents—often making a dangerous, even life threatening,

States with the Most Mexican Americans

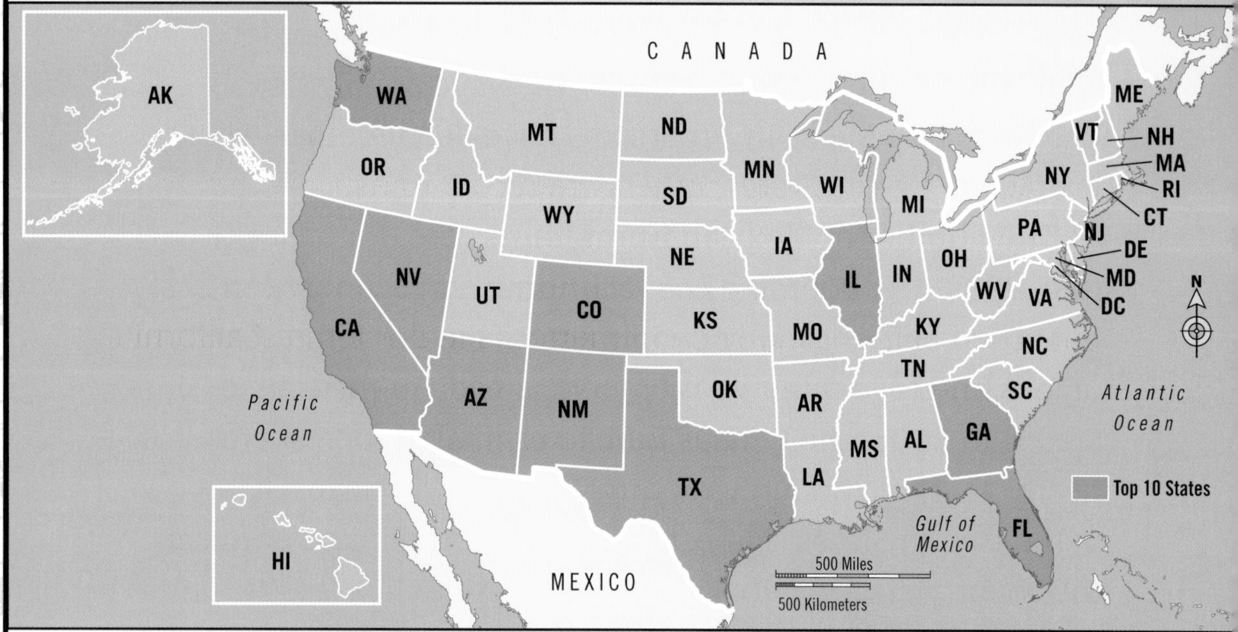

California	10,841,524
Texas	7,024,667
Arizona	1,601,082
Illinois	1,486,386
Colorado	671,341
Florida	563,110
Nevada	475,390
Washington	464,652
Georgia	455,008
New Mexico	448,714

Source: U.S. Bureau of the Census, 2006 estimates

journey to try to get across the border without being detected by U.S. officials. Some of these **undocumented** immigrants were from other countries (for example, Central American countries). Many came from Mexico. Tighter security along the border, combined with economic troubles in the United States, has led to a small decline of undocumented immigration since 2005. Nevertheless, the extent of undocumented immigration has sparked a major debate in the United States about immigration policy.

Where Mexican Americans Live

More than half of all Mexican Americans live in either California or Texas. Other states with historically high populations of Mexican Americans include New Mexico and Arizona. Mexican immigrants are still drawn to both states.

But significant numbers of Mexican Americans now live in all parts of the United States. In recent years, large numbers of Mexican immigrants have settled in Illinois (especially the Chicago area) in the Midwest, in Florida and Georgia in the Southeast, and in Colorado, Nevada, and Washington in the West.

Deep Impact

For much of their long history in the United States, Mexican Americans have faced **prejudice** and **discrimination** because of skin color or language or both. They have been the victims of negative **stereotypes**. At the same time, Mexican Americans and their culture have had an important and long-lasting impact on much of the Southwest—and more recently on the rest of the United States as well. Mexican-Americans are a vital part of the culture, politics, and economy of the United States today.

Founded in 1769, Mission San Diego de Alcala was the first of a series of missions established throughout what is now California by Spanish missionaries from Mexico.

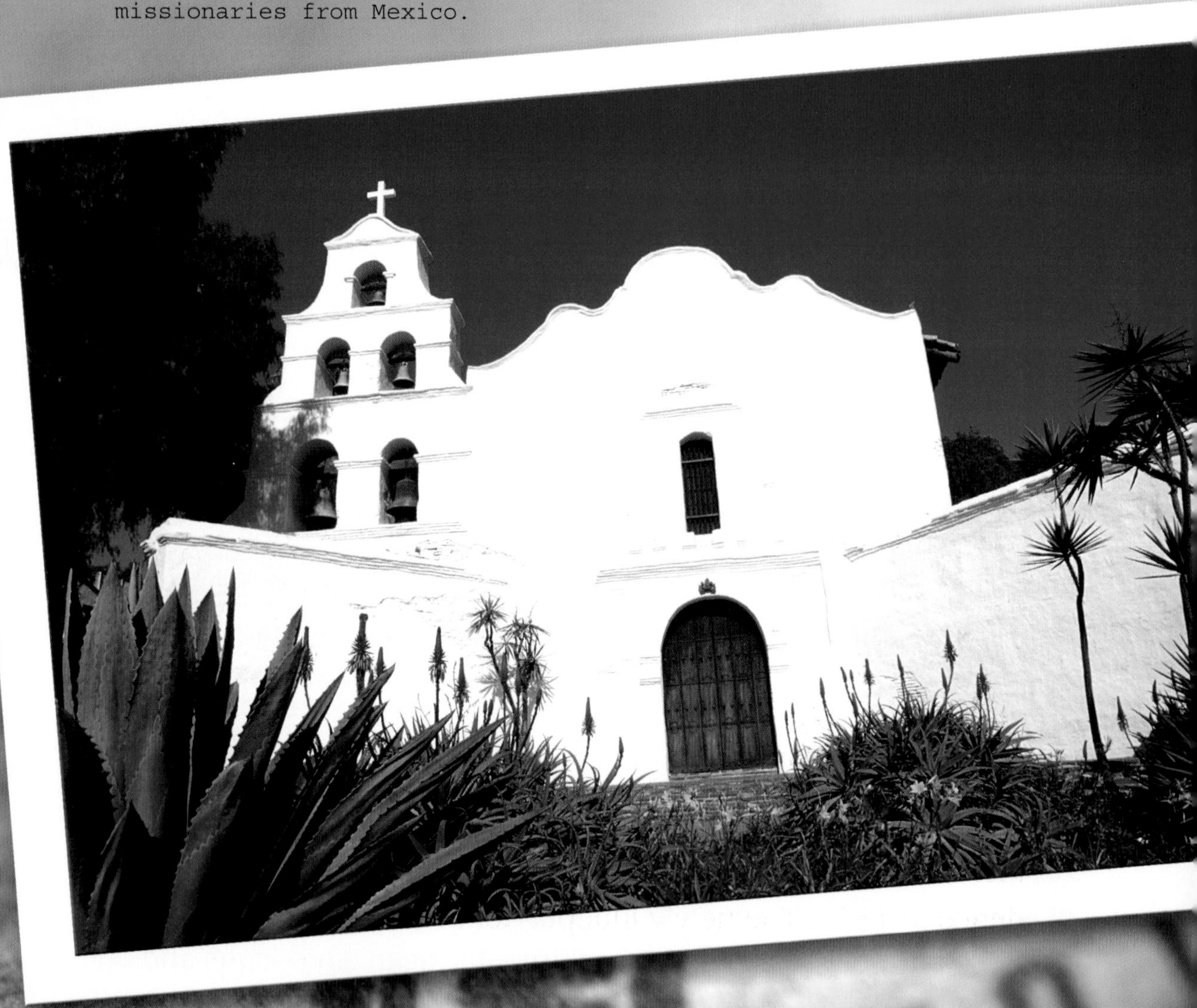

CHAPTER TWO

EARLIER GENERATIONS

Because what is now the U.S. Southwest was once part of Mexico, it can be said that to a large extent, the first Mexicans to become residents of the United States did so not because they crossed the border, but because the border crossed them. Border changes occurred in three steps in the mid-1800s.

The Texas Rebellion

Mexico was controlled by Spain until it won its independence in 1821. The newly independent Mexican government welcomed settlers from the United States into Texas, which was then very sparsely populated. Also in 1821, the American trader and former military officer William Becknell opened what became known as the Santa Fe Trail, a wagon route from Missouri to the settlement of Santa Fe in the Mexican province of New Mexico. Although at first used mostly to transport goods for trade, the Santa Fe Trail eventually became a major route for U.S. settlers heading to the Southwest.

By the early 1830s, some 20,000 people from the United States had settled in Texas. Some of these settlers, especially those who had come from the slave states of the South, introduced slavery in Texas. Many Caucasian Americans saw Texas as a paradise just waiting to be developed. As the famous frontiersman Davy Crockett wrote in an 1836 letter to his daughter and son-in-law:

> "I must say as to what I have seen of Texas, it is the garden spot of the world. The best land and best prospects for health I ever saw, and I do so believe it is a fortune to any man to come here. There is a world of country to settle."

Being under Mexican rule did not sit well with the growing number of U.S. settlers, particularly after the Mexican government imposed new taxes and tried to abolish slavery. In 1835, led by Sam Houston and others, the U.S. settlers rebelled against Mexico, and early the next year, they declared Texas an independent republic. Mexican dictator Antonio Lopez de Santa Anna responded to the rebellion by leading an army north into Texas. One of the bloodiest battles took place in March 1836 at the Alamo, a fort (and former mission) in San Antonio. It ended with the Mexican forces defeating and killing the outnumbered Texans and other defenders, including Davy Crockett. "Remember the Alamo!" became a battle cry for the

Timeline: Texas, California, and the Southwest Join the United States	
1519–1521	Spanish explorer Hernán Cortés and his army conquer the Aztecs and other native groups and establish Spanish control over what is now Mexico.
1598	Spanish settlers from Mexico begin to establish settlements in New Mexico, founding the city of Santa Fe in 1610.
1682	Spanish Franciscan priests from Mexico begin to establish the first Spanish missions and settlements in Texas.
1769	Spanish Franciscan priests and settlers from Mexico begin to establish missions and settlements in California, founding the city of Los Angeles in 1781.
1821	Mexico gains independence from Spain. William Becknell establishes the Santa Fe Trail, linking Missouri and the Southwest. Mexico allows Stephen F. Austin to start American settlements in Texas.
1836	Texas wins its independence from Mexico.
1845	The United States annexes Texas.
1846–1848	The United States defeats Mexico in the Mexican-American War.
1848	In the Treaty of Guadalupe Hidalgo, which ends the Mexican-American War, the United States obtains from Mexico the territory of California and the vast province of New Mexico in the Southwest.
1853	The Gadsden Purchase alters the U.S.-Mexican border one last time. For $10 million, the United States acquires from Mexico about 30,000 square miles (78,000 square kilometers) of land in what is now southern Arizona and New Mexico.

Led by General Zachary Taylor, U.S. forces who had invaded Mexico defeated Mexican troops at the Battle of Buena Vista in 1847, during the Mexican-American War.

Texans, and in April 1836, an army led by Sam Houston defeated Santa Anna's army at the Battle of San Jacinto. Santa Anna himself was captured, and he recognized the independence of Texas.

Manifest Destiny

In the mid–1800s, many Americans believed that it was their country's "manifest destiny" (that is, clearly evident destiny) to expand its territory. U.S. President James Polk, who took office in 1845, was one of them. Polk believed that enlarging the country would make the nation safer from foreign attacks, provide new land for settlement, and increase prosperity. Polk favored annexing Texas, and it became a U.S. state in 1845. But the Mexican government at that time did not recognize Santa Anna's grant of independence to Texas. Mexican officials also disputed with the United States where the western boundary of Texas should be located, and they refused Polk's offer to purchase California and the province of New Mexico.

Perhaps seeking to provoke a war, Polk sent U.S. troops to the disputed Texas border area. When Mexican forces attacked these troops, the United States declared war on Mexico. The Mexican-American War (1846–1848) ended in victory for the United States. In the resulting Treaty of Guadalupe Hidalgo, Mexico gave up all claims to Texas and agreed to give California and New Mexico to the United States in exchange for $15 million. The treaty allowed Mexicans living in this new U.S. territory to become U.S. citizens if they chose.

In 1853, the U.S.-Mexico border changed to what it is today when the United States purchased from Mexico a strip of land in what is now southern New Mexico and Arizona. It wanted the land to complete a new railroad to California. James Gadsden, U.S. minister (ambassador) to Mexico, negotiated this so-called Gadsden Purchase of about 30,000 square miles (78,000 square kilometers) of land for $10 million.

Building the Border

The U.S.-Mexico border as it has existed since 1853 stretches for some 2,000 miles (3,200 kilometers). Four

In the 1840s and 1850s, huge areas that had once been part of Mexico became part of the United States with the annexation of Texas, the U.S. victory over Mexico in the Mexican-American War, and the Gadsden Purchase.

U.S. states—from west to east, California, Arizona, New Mexico, and Texas—share a border with Mexico. The border was originally marked off rather haphazardly. Often its location was marked by nothing more than a pile of rocks or a railroad spike driven into the ground. Many people just ignored it. In fact, one man in Arizona in the late 1880s built his tavern around a pile of rocks that was a border marker, so that the marker stood inside his saloon. In the late nineteenth century, more markers were added. Still, figuring out exactly where the boundary fell was like playing a game of connect the dots.

This mostly open border was often crossed by people who moved back and forth between the two countries with ease. Most people at that time did not think of the border as a barrier to freedom of movement. Many Mexican families had members on both sides of the border.

Border Crossings

The early twentieth century brought the first large wave of Mexican immigrants. The U.S. economy was booming, and jobs were plentiful. Mexico, on the other hand, was gripped by revolution from 1910 to 1920, and many Mexicans went north to escape the social and economic upheaval. According to U.S. government estimates, about half a million Mexicans entered the United States between 1910 and 1920. The actual number may have been much higher than

The Treaty of Guadalupe Hidalgo and U.S. Citizenship

Article VIII of the Treaty of Guadalupe Hidalgo that ended the Mexican-American War in 1848 provided a way for Mexicans living in California and the Southwest to become U.S. citizens when this area became part of the United States. The Article stated, in part:

> "Mexicans now established in territories previously belonging to Mexico, and which remain for the future within the limits of the United States, as defined by the present treaty, shall be free to continue where they now reside, or to remove at any time to the Mexican Republic. . . .
>
> "Those who shall prefer to remain in the said territories may either retain the title and rights of Mexican citizens, or acquire those of citizens of the United States. But they shall be under the obligation to make their election within one year from the date of the exchange of ratifications of this treaty; and those who shall remain in the said territories after the expiration of that year, without having declared their intention to retain the character of Mexicans, shall be considered to have elected to become citizens of the United States."

that. Since the border was so open, the exact number can't be known.

The U.S. government enacted a number of laws in the early twentieth century to regulate and control immigration. A 1917 law said that immigrants had to be able to read (in any language) in order to enter the country and had to pay a fee. Since many Mexicans entering the United States at that time were poor and illiterate, they simply crossed the largely open border after the law was passed without going through the immigration process and getting approval to enter. In 1924, Congress created the U.S. Border Patrol to police the border, but it started out with just 450 officers, far from enough to adequately do the job.

The Border Patrol was established in the same year that Congress passed the Immigration Act of 1924. This new law generally sought to limit immigration to the United States. It set quotas, or limits, on the number of immigrants allowed to enter each year from most countries in the world. The act set no quotas, however, for Mexico and other countries in the Americas. Mexican workers were

A Mexican-American Political First

U.S. expansion to include former Mexican regions changed the culture and the politics of the United States. Presidential candidates now tried to appeal to Mexican-American voters, and Mexican Americans began running for office. José Antonio Romualdo Pacheco Jr. (1831–1899) was the first Hispanic to become governor of California. Pacheco was of Mexican descent, but he was also the first California governor to be born in the state. His thirty-year career in politics took him from California's state senate to the governor's office in 1875. He went on to serve three terms in the U.S. House of Representatives. Although he was not the first Hispanic to serve in the U.S. House, he was the first to have full voting rights because he represented a state and not a U.S. territory.

seen as an important part of the work force in the United States. Many Mexicans came to the United States to work seasonally, on farms for example, and then returned home to Mexico.

Border Ballads

Mexican immigrants crossing the border in the early twentieth century told of their experiences in songs called border ballads. This one talks of the sadness a Mexican immigrant feels leaving his home country:

Ballad of an Immigrant

Mexico, my homeland, where I was born,
Give me the benediction of your powerful hand,
I'm going to the United States to earn my living,
Good-bye, my beloved country, I carry you in my heart,
Don't condemn me for leaving my country,
Poverty and necessity are at fault.
Good-bye, pretty Guanajuato, the state in which I was born,
I'm going to the United States far away from you.

The Great Depression

The Great Depression, which began in 1929 and continued through the 1930s, was a period of severe economic

Workers rebuild a border marker along the U.S.-Mexico border in the 1890s.

Migrant workers pick carrots in a California field in the 1930s. When it was available, the work was hard and the pay low.

hardship in the United States. Businesses failed, and millions of people lost their jobs. Also in the 1930s, a drought in the Midwest brought ruin to many family farms. The Depression hit Mexican Americans particularly hard. Many of them worked as laborers and as farm workers, and large numbers of those jobs disappeared. At the same time, widespread unemployment gave rise to anti-immigrant **sentiment**. Many people resented having to compete with immigrants for jobs that were in short supply.

As there was no longer a need for a large immigrant labor pool, the U.S. government began to **deport** Mexican immigrants on a massive scale. The exact number of people deported from the United States to Mexico during this time is not known. Estimates range from 400,000 to 2 million. Local immigration officials and police circulated stories about deportation "raids" as a way of frightening people into leaving. Those who left voluntarily at least had time to collect their belongings.

Others were rounded up by authorities and forced onto trains or trucks bound for Mexico with little more than the clothes on their backs. Forced **repatriation** reached its peak in 1931. The mass deportation included documented and undocumented immigrants; it included temporary workers and permanent residents. Some of the Mexican Americans who were forcibly deported were U.S. citizens, including children who were born in the United States. People who are born on U.S. soil are automatically granted citizenship status.

Voices from the Dust Bowl

In 1940, Augustus Martinez lived in a migrant work camp in El Rio, California. He was one of many migrant workers interviewed by Charles L. Todd and Robert Sonkin of the City College of New York, who were documenting the life and times of so-called "Dust Bowl refugees." In this interview, Martinez talks about the ways in which the local Mexican-American community was organizing politically:

> "Here in Ventura County, we're trying to . . . get the young folks united and trying to be respected . . . by getting together and showing them what an American citizen's privileges are and how we can use them. . . . At the same time it gives us a more powerful arm, so we can defend ourselves, you know. . . . If we get together and vote, we can show them that we've got something to talk about, because the government of the United States is something that respects everybody, and if you work hard, according to the laws, why, there is no difference in the government [no matter what] race you are. Discrimination comes from most of the people around here. . . . We're just set down lower than we should be."

Hard Day's Work

Jesús Campoya Calderón, from the state of Chihuahua in Mexico, came to the United States in 1951 as part of the Bracero program. He worked on farms in New Mexico and Texas. He described his experience as follows:

> "In the farms we would do anything, although our permit was to pick cotton only. . . .Because I did not trust the bank, I saved all my money myself. I worked four months, seven days a week, at least 12 hours every day, and I took home $300. . . .Those were very good days."

To find work during the Depression, some Mexican Americans moved from rural areas to nearby cities such as Los Angeles and San Antonio. Large Mexican-American communities grew up in many cities of the Southwest. Today, these thriving communities are often a first destination for new immigrants—a place where people speak their language and share their customs and where the newcomers can feel "at home."

Other Mexican Americans during the Depression looked for work in the automobile factories and steel mills of Detroit and Chicago. Those cities saw a significant increase in their Mexican-American populations in the 1930s.

Still other Mexican Americans moved into migrant work camps set up by the U.S. Farm Security Administration. The camps offered housing, food, medical care, and protection for migrant families. The families living in the camps formed close-knit communities. Importantly, they also began to form political organizations for the first time to fight discrimination and push for greater civil rights. The League of United Latin American Citizens (LULAC), formed in 1929, was one such group. It encouraged eligible immigrants to become U.S. citizens and be politically active. It also worked for better economic and educational opportunities for all Hispanics.

Guest Workers Welcome

By the end of the 1930s, the United States once again welcomed Mexican immigrants. While the United States fought in World War II from 1941 to 1945, millions of men were in the armed forces (including hundreds of thousands of Mexican Americans; Mexican Americans were awarded thirty Congressional Medals of Honor for their service during the war). There was a huge need for workers in factories and on farms. To meet the need, the United States and Mexico created the so-called Bracero program (the name comes from the Spanish word *brazo*, which means "arm"). This program allowed Mexicans to come to the United States under temporary work permits. Farmers' organizations and the U.S. government found the workers jobs that matched their skills. Started in 1942, the program continued after World War II, running until 1964. It was the longest running guest worker program in U.S. history.

Most of the braceros found work on farms, planting and picking crops. After a long day working in the fields, the braceros were often given additional work, mending fences or doing other odd jobs for which they were not paid. Still, they made more money than they would have in Mexico. The Bracero program attracted some 4 million Mexicans to the United States. Agricultural development in the Southwest would not have been possible without their hard work. Many of them returned to Mexico when their work permits expired. Some, however, stayed and continued to live in the United States without documentation.

Also, as it became clear that a worker could make more money as a farm laborer in the United States than he or she could make in Mexico, many Mexicans began simply crossing the border without authorization and going directly to the owners of large farms to seek work. Many growers welcomed these new laborers—and also took advantage of their undocumented status by paying especially low wages and not providing decent working conditions.

Racial Tensions Mount

Mexican immigrants had long been the victims of discrimination. Many Americans stereotyped them as lazy, dirty, uneducated, or even criminal and often barred them from entry into "whites only" areas in theaters and restaurants. In the early 1940s, racial tensions grew violent in Los Angeles, where the Mexican-American population topped 250,000.

Mexican-American teenagers were particular targets. They were often called "zooters," a name that came from the fashionable zoot suits they wore. A zoot suit featured baggy pants that tapered at the ankles and a long tight-fitting jacket with padded shoulders. It was the height of fashion for young Mexican Americans, but many people thought the Mexican-American teens were showing off at a time when everyone was encouraged to cut back on luxuries to help the war effort. To many, the zoot-suited teens seemed unpatriotic and uncaring about the war.

Clashes between Mexican-American teenagers and American servicemen on leave in Los Angeles became increasingly common. The youths would sometimes attack drunken soldiers who came to party in their neighborhoods. Other times, servicemen would attack the teens. Los Angeles police officers also clashed with Mexican-American youths, whom the police often viewed as gang members. Many Mexican American teens felt

These two young men were attacked during the Zoot Suit Riots in Los Angeles in 1943.

A Plea for Fairness

In 1942, the Youth Committee for the Defense of Mexican American Youth sent a letter to Vice President Henry A. Wallace. This is what, in part, it said:

> "We are writing you this letter because we heard you speak on the 16th of September here in Los Angeles, and we feel you should know about the bad situation facing us Mexican boys and girls and our whole Spanish-speaking community. . . .
>
> "In our neighborhood there are no recreation centers, and the nearest movie is about a mile away. We have no place to play so the Police are always arresting us . . . and searching us by the hundreds when all we want to do is go into a dance or go swimming or just stand around and not bother anybody. They treat us like we are criminals just by being Mexicans or of Mexican descent. The newspapers have made us look like criminals too. They make fun of zoot suits and use the word 'Mexicans' like it was a dirty word. . . .
>
> "Discrimination is what hurts the most . . . because discrimination is the thing that makes the other Americans divide from us."

unfairly targeted by the police, who would typically arrest them and not the servicemen when breaking up a fight. In 1943, the frequent fights between American servicemen and young Mexican Americans in the Los Angeles area erupted in what were called the Zoot Suit Riots. For days, mobs of servicemen carrying clubs attacked every Mexican-American man or boy they found.

¡Sí, Se Puede! **(Yes, We Can!)**

The 1960s saw the creation of many powerful civil rights organizations, including the Mexican American Legal Defense and Educational Fund, started in 1968. By far the best known largely Mexican-American organization, however, is the United Farm Workers of America (UFW), which was founded in 1962. The group's first leader was Cesar Chavez, a Mexican American who grew up—first in Arizona and then

Cesar Chavez *(right)* and other picketers march outside a New Jersey supermarket in 1974, urging shoppers not to buy lettuce and grapes.

in California—in a family of migrant farm workers. He formed the UFW union to push for better pay and working conditions for agricultural laborers in California and the Southwest, many of whom toiled in the fields for long hours without breaks, water, or even access to bathrooms.

Chavez was inspired by civil rights leader Martin Luther King Jr., as well as others, and was committed to achieving the UFW's goals without violence. In the 1960s and 1970s, he led strikes against grape and vegetable growers. The strikers' rallying cry was "*¡Sí, se puede!*" ("Yes, we can!"). He also organized successful nationwide **boycotts** against buying grapes and lettuce to support the UFW's goals. By the late 1970s, most growers had signed contracts with the UFW that gave farm laborers better working conditions, health-care benefits, and pensions.

Signs are in Spanish and restaurants try to appeal to Mexican-American customers in this Hispanic neighborhood in Chicago.

CHAPTER THREE

THE NEW IMMIGRANTS

The late twentieth century saw a significant increase in immigration from Mexico to the United States. According to U.S. Immigration and Naturalization Service statistics, 2.2 million documented Mexican immigrants entered the United States in the 1990s, making up 12 percent of all documented immigrants in that decade. The number of undocumented immigrants may have been even higher.

The surge in immigrants, both documented and undocumented, was driven largely by economic factors. In general, the booming U.S. economy offered more opportunities than Mexico's struggling economy, which suffered a series of financial crises in the 1980s and 1990s.

In addition, in 1994 the United States, Mexico, and Canada signed the North American Free Trade Agreement (NAFTA), a pact aimed at increasing trade between the three countries by eliminating **tariffs** and other fees on goods shipped across national borders. Supporters of NAFTA predicted that it would stimulate the Mexican economy, increase employment opportunities in Mexico, and reduce the number of immigrants coming from Mexico to the

Workers make clothing at a garment factory in California. As the number of jobs in the state's garment industry has decreased, more Mexican immigrants have sought work in other parts of the United States.

United States. But while the agreement led to an increase in factory jobs, especially in parts of Mexico near the U.S. border, poor people in the Mexican countryside saw little benefit. Under NAFTA, the Mexican government stopped giving payments called **subsidies** to farmers who grew staple crops (foods, such as corn, that make up a large part of the typical person's diet). Instead, the government began importing low-cost corn and other crops from the United States. That drove many Mexican farmers out of business, and it made food more expensive for the many Mexican consumers who already were barely scraping by.

Mexico's rising prices, high interest rates, and large national debt led to an economic crisis in 1995. The value of the peso, Mexico's currency, dropped dramatically. There was also political instability at this time, including the assassination of a presidential candidate in 1994. In response, many Mexicans left to seek work in the United States. Their wages, paid in U.S. dollars, were worth far more than their earnings would have been in Mexico.

Seeking Opportunity in New Places

A high level of immigration, both documented and undocumented, continued in the first years of the twenty-first century. By this time, though, significant numbers of the new immigrants from Mexico did not head for California, Texas, or other traditional settlement states for Mexican arrivals. Among the reasons: housing costs in these areas were rising and job opportunities were shrinking. The garment industry, for example, once a major employer for Mexican

Americans in Los Angeles, was closing factories and sending work overseas.

Instead, many twenty-first century Mexican immigrants have found job opportunities in so-called new settlement states, including Massachusetts, Virginia, North Carolina, Georgia, Nevada, Oregon, and Washington. These immigrants, like those who came before them, took jobs primarily in agriculture, construction, and manufacturing. But instead of sewing clothes in Los Angeles, they were working, for example, in carpet factories in Dalton, Georgia.

Another reason newer immigrants have been going to new settlement states is tighter border security. As it became more difficult in recent years for undocumented immigrants to cross near—and look for work in—densely populated areas of California and Texas, many tried crossing the border elsewhere and then moving on to look for work in the new settlement states.

Tightening the Border

The U.S. government began in the 1980s to intensify efforts to tighten security and reduce undocumented immigration along the U.S.-Mexico border. A growing number of Americans became concerned that new immigrants were competing for jobs and placing a strain on social services, such as hospitals and schools, and elected officials responded. The Immigration Reform and Control Act of 1986 created penalties for employers who hired undocumented immigrants and increased the size of the Border Patrol. As undocumented immigration continued, some fencing was put up in popular crossing areas and intensive enforcement operations were begun in these areas, including "Operation Hold the Line" near El Paso, Texas, and "Operation Gate-keeper" near San Diego, California.

After the September 11, 2001, terrorist attacks against the United States, border security became a national priority. There was a concern that terrorists could enter the country by crossing the U.S.-Mexico border, and the Border Patrol was again expanded. Cameras, motion sensors, and other electronic **surveillance** devices were installed in some areas. In 2006, Congress approved a measure to build a total of about 700 miles (1,100 kilometers) of fences along stretches of the U.S.-Mexico border. Collectively, the fences would create barriers across about one-third

New security fences, like this one near San Diego, have made it more difficult for undocumented immigrants to cross the border near major cities in California or Texas.

of the entire border. By early 2009, more than 600 miles (965 kilometers) of this fencing had been constructed.

All of these efforts have reduced the number of undocumented immigrants in recent years. The border has remained porous, however, with people continuing to find ways to pass back and forth between the two countries. One of these ways is crossing the border at different, more remote locations—including crossing the desert into Arizona. The extremely harsh conditions can make this crossing a potentially deadly undertaking.

Deadly Journey

During the scorching summer months, temperatures in the Sonoran Desert, which spans both sides of the Mexico-Arizona border, can top

Charitable organizations put out water barrels in the Arizona desert, to aid immigrants crossing the desert in the scorching heat.

125°F (52°C). In winter, nighttime temperatures frequently fall to well below freezing. Many immigrants are not prepared for such conditions. Without enough water and appropriate clothing to sustain them, many people die. It's hard to say exactly how many undocumented immigrants die while trying to get into the United States in this way—bodies may go undiscovered for some time in that wide expanse of desert. Most of the bodies that are discovered in that area are those of undocumented immigrants between the ages of fifteen and forty.

Charitable organizations have intervened in an effort to reduce the death toll. One such group is Humane Borders, a federation of volunteers from churches and immigrant rights organizations, which has set up more than eighty water stations around the Arizona desert. Some of these locations also supply immigrants with food, first aid kits, and warm clothing in winter. The water barrels are plastic, painted blue, and have the word *agua* (Spanish for "water") painted on the side. "We're holding up a mirror to society," the Reverend Robin Hoover, Humane Borders' leader, said in an interview with the *Los Angeles Times*. "We're saying that we are all, all of us, responsible for what is happening out here."

Beware of Coyotes!

Because of the risks involved in taking the undocumented route from Mexico to the United States—even before the most recent tightening of border controls—some people pay smugglers, known as **coyotes**, to help them sneak

Two coyotes take immigrants across the Rio Grande from Mexico into Texas.

across the border. But these smugglers often cannot be trusted. Some may take the immigrants' money and then just abandon them in a remote area, or at least abandon anyone who becomes too ill or tired to keep going.

In one extreme case, in May 2003, sheriffs made a grisly discovery in a sealed tractor trailer at a truck stop near Victoria, Texas. At least seventy-four Mexicans and Central Americans had paid smugglers to sneak them across the border from Mexico. Once in Texas, however, the smugglers abandoned the trailer, leaving the immigrants trapped inside. As temperatures in the trailer soared to 100°F (38°C) and beyond, some of the immigrants suffocated. Others died of heat stroke. Desperate for air, the immigrants had bored holes in the side of the trailer. Ultimately, someone heard their cries for help and called 911.

One Person's Story: Maria Hernandez

Maria Hernandez was only a child when her parents brought her across the border from Mexico in the 1980s. She tells the story of her dangerous journey as an undocumented immigrant on Energy of a Nation, a website for immigrants set up by The Advocates for Human Rights, a nonprofit organization that assists immigrants in Minnesota:

"I was born in Mexico, but I have lived much of my life in the United States. I am fifteen years old.

"When I was a baby, my dad moved to the United States to find work. Later, he saved enough money to pay a coyote to help smuggle my mom, brothers, and me into the United States. I remember going to the coyote's house near the border, dressing in dark clothing, and being told by my mom to be very quiet. I was very scared crossing the river, because we had to cross the river in the boat one at a time, and I was the last one in my family to cross the river with the coyote and I was afraid I was going to be left behind. Eventually we made our way into the United States, where we have lived together for years. My parents and I were granted **amnesty** in the early 1990s and we all have our **green cards** now. ["Green card" is the informal name for the document that proves an immigrant has U.S. government authorization to be a permanent resident of the United States.]

"My mom and dad have worked as farm workers since we came to the United States. For most of my childhood, we have lived in Texas, Arizona, and California in the winter and Minnesota in the summer. Sometimes I get to go to school, but I have often had to help my family at work or watch my brothers and sisters. This is the first year we are staying in Minnesota for the winter, because my mom and dad have jobs all year round."

Rescuers arrived to find seventeen people dead, including a seven-year-old boy. One man died after being taken to the hospital, bringing the total death toll to eighteen. The disaster remains one of the deadliest incidents of human smuggling in the United States. "This grim discovery is a horrific reminder of the callous disregard smugglers have for their human cargo," said Asa Hutchinson, then the undersecretary for border and transportation security for the U.S. Department of Homeland Security.

Separation Anxiety

Because of the risks, some men with families make the trek alone to find work as undocumented immigrants in the United States (though this has become less common in recent years). When a husband travels alone, the family members who stayed behind often must depend on whatever money the breadwinner sends back to Mexico. In part because many are undocumented, Mexican immigrants tend to experience longer periods of family separation than other immigrant groups in the United States. The undocumented cannot go home for a visit and be sure they will get back safely across the border. Nor can they be sure they will have a job in the United States when they return. Some may be away from their families for years. Because of these difficulties, a growing number of women are deciding to cross the border and join their husbands in the United States. One study estimated that in 2006, about 35 percent of new undocumented immigrants from Mexico were adult women.

Even for legal immigrants, the process of bringing family members to join them in the United States is slow, complicated, and expensive. Immigrants with little money and little education often have difficulty understanding the process and filling out the forms needed to obtain a visa. One error means they are bumped to the back of the line and have to reapply. So the process may take years. In addition, because many immigrants work for low wages and send money home each month, it's hard for them to save the several thousand dollars needed for visa application fees and to pay travel and moving expenses.

The number of visas available each year to people from all countries is limited by U.S. law. To encourage the reunification of families, a portion of the available visas are set aside to allow legal permanent residents to bring immediate family members to the United States. In addition, for U.S. citizens there are no limits on the number of immediate family members—a wife or husband, unmarried children under twenty-one, and parents—they can bring to join them. Nevertheless, because of immigration backlogs, the wait for a visa can last for years. Such delays lead some family members to cross without documents to reunite families. The long delays can pose a particular problem for parents trying to bring teenagers to join them in the United States, because the children must be under twenty-one when they arrive in order to be entitled to entry. Fearful that they will run out of time taking the legal route, some people feel they have no choice but to bring their teenage children into the United States without documentation.

The Plight of Children

Each year, U.S. authorities catch about 43,000 unaccompanied minors trying to cross the border without documentation. Teenagers and other undocumented minor children are vulnerable to mistreatment, and not only at the hands of coyotes. A study released in November 2008 by the Center for Public Policy, an Austin, Texas–based policy and research organization, found they also suffered at the hands of U.S. authorities. The study found that some children were handcuffed and went without water and medical treatment at U.S. Border Patrol stations. Although they faced complicated legal charges, 50 to 70 percent had no lawyers to represent them when they went before an immigration judge. Mexican officials reported that children were often returned to the wrong destinations in Mexico and that officials weren't always notified when children were being returned. Many of the children reported they were trying to join their parents in the United States.

Mexican immigrants take an ESL (English as a second language) class at a branch of the University of Texas in Brownsville.

CHAPTER FOUR

MAKING A NEW LIFE

Why are so many Mexican immigrants willing to risk their lives to come to the United States? The answer is that many view the United States as a land of freedom and opportunities—a place where they might have a shot at a better life. That was what earlier immigrants—including the Europeans who braved the stormy Atlantic Ocean—believed. That is why Mexicans brave the heat of the desert.

For poor Mexicans, the United States offers the promise of higher paying jobs than they can find in their native country. It also offers their children the promise of a better education and a brighter future.

Hard Work for Low Pay

In general, Mexicans who come to the United States tend to be poorer than immigrants from many other countries. Most immigrants from Asia, for instance, must at least be able to afford airfare to the United States. The poorest Mexican, however, can simply walk across the border. But those who enter the country without money or a visa face several obstacles.

Undocumented workers have little choice but to take whatever work they can find. Many are exploited by employers, who make them work long hours for low wages, often in unsafe conditions. Few complain, however, because they don't want to risk losing their jobs. Also, they cannot complain to government agencies that protect workers' rights because they don't want to attract the attention of immigration authorities.

Indeed, many feel lucky to have jobs. The unemployment rate for Mexican-American immigrants is believed to be higher than the jobless rate for Americans as a whole. But accurate figures are difficult to determine because undocumented immigrants tend to be part of the United States' vast "underground" workforce. Many work as day laborers who are hired to do short-term jobs and are paid in cash. There are no official records of their employment, and the workers are not entitled to unemployment payments or other benefits that appear on public records.

Employers who hire undocumented immigrants are violating U.S. law, and some pay a price for doing so. In May 2008, for instance, immigration officials raided a meat-processing plant in Iowa. Plant operators were accused of employing nearly 400 undocumented workers. Among them were thirty-two children under age eighteen, including seven who were younger than sixteen. Many had been exposed to hazardous chemicals and dangerous machines, such as meat grinders and circular saws. In September 2008, the Iowa attorney general filed criminal charges against the plant's owners for more than 9,300 child labor law violations.

The immigration authorities also arrested hundreds of workers during the raid. The workers were charged with being in the United States illegally and committing other crimes, such as using fake Social Security numbers or real ones that weren't theirs.

Many Mexican immigrants take low-paying jobs in restaurants and other service businesses.

Language Barriers

"Everyone in the world smiles in the same language" is a popular proverb among Mexican Americans. It's hard to get by on just a smile, though. Many Mexican-American immigrants find that their imperfect English-language skills limit their opportunities in the United States. In 2006, the U.S. Census Bureau reported that 41 percent of Mexican Americans said they spoke English less than "very well." About 80 percent of Mexican Americans said they spoke mostly Spanish at home.

Many adult immigrants rely on their children to translate for them, once these children have learned English in school. This is very helpful for the families, but it puts children in the position of translating conversations about "grown-up" topics, such as legal or medical issues.

Moving Up in the World

More than one in four foreign-born workers in the United States comes from Mexico. However, Mexican immigrants work mostly in lower-paying jobs that offer limited opportunities for advancement. In 2006, about 23 percent were service workers, mostly in restaurants and hotels. Another 20 percent worked in production, transportation, and material-moving occupations (primarily for railroads, factories, and trucking companies). And some 19 percent had jobs in construction, mining, maintenance, and repair occupations.

Some studies have found that it takes longer for Mexican Americans to become upwardly mobile than other immigrants. In one 1990 study, researchers found that only 19 percent of first generation Mexican-American men had moved beyond low-wage jobs. First generation Mexican-American women (who, on average, had more years of schooling) fared somewhat better, the study found, with 31 percent of women making strides in the working world. Seventeen percent of them had jobs in professional and technical fields, compared with 9 percent of the men. (People are generally considered "first generation" if their parents were born elsewhere and immigrated to the United States.)

English Only?

Most schools with large numbers of students who know little English offer special classes for such students. These ESL (English as a second language) or ELL (English-language learner) classes are intended to teach the students English. But what happens to these students in other parts of the school day, when they are supposed to be learning math, or history, or science? In what language should they be taught those subjects? Different states have answered that question differently. Some, including Texas, have provided for dual-language instruction, allowing for Spanish-speaking students to be taught academic subjects in their native language until their English improves. Other states, including California and Arizona, have taken a different approach, requiring that the language of instruction in academic subjects must be English. Educators and others continue to debate which of these approaches may be better for students who are English-language learners.

The job picture features some encouraging statistics, however. In 2006, 14 percent of Mexican Americans (both men and women) were employed in business or professional fields; another 20 percent had office jobs or worked in sales.

Family Matters

On average, Mexican Americans are less affluent than Americans as a whole. The median income for Mexican-

American families in 2006 was about $38,000—more than $20,000 less than the figure for all American families. In the same year, 23 percent of Mexican Americans were living below the poverty level (as defined by the U.S. government), compared to 13 percent for the U.S. population as a whole.

Mexican-American workers tend to have larger households to support than many other workers. In 2006, the average Mexican-American family size was about four people, compared to about three for American families as a whole. Just over half of Mexican-American families have children under eighteen. In fact, more than one-third of all

Children at work at an elementary school in Texas, a state that allows dual-language instruction because of its many Spanish-speaking students.

Mexican Americans are under eighteen (compared to one-quarter for the entire U.S. population).

School-age children who are immigrants may have their own challenges. Those who enter school speaking little or no English can have a great deal of trouble keeping up with schoolwork while they master a new language. If the family works in agriculture and moves each crop-growing season, the children may face extra challenges: they must switch schools frequently, as well as make new friends, and try to catch up with work they may have missed. Keeping up with schoolwork is even more difficult for teens who have to work in the fields alongside their parents. Others stay home to look after younger siblings while their parents work two jobs to make ends meet.

Mexican-American teens can be torn between these competing needs to get an education and to help support their family. High school dropout rates for Mexican Americans are higher than for American teenagers as a whole. In 2006, almost half (46 percent) of Mexican Americans age twenty-five or older had no high school diploma (compared to 16 percent for all adult Americans), and only 8 percent of adult Mexican Americans had a college degree (compared to 27 percent for all Americans).

A 2007 study of Mexican-American high school students in Omaha, Nebraska, found that most foreign-born students said they had to work to help support their family. Many of them worked alongside their parents, typically in low-skilled jobs at local meatpacking plants. Most of these students said they planned to finish high school. But only 16 percent said that most people they knew at school planned to go to college (teenagers whose peers intend to go to college are more likely to go themselves).

The situation does improve somewhat over the generations. In the 2007 Omaha study, about one-third of first-generation Mexican-American teens said most students they knew planned to go to college. Only 18 percent of the first-generation Mexican Americans said they had to work to help support their families.

Mexican-American teens, like most teens, want to fit in with their peers. Yet their parents' values and traditions may be quite different from those of their friends. Some Mexican-born parents may not approve of their teenage daughters dating or going out without an adult along.

Mexican-American children born and raised in the United States face another problem: they may be unfairly categorized as undocumented immigrants even though they are citizens. At the same time, they face the anti-immigrant sentiments and negative stereotypes that have haunted Mexican Americans for decades.

Deportation Fears

Many undocumented immigrants live in fear of being discovered by authorities. These fears are well-founded. In 2008, U.S. Immigration and Customs Enforcement, a division of the Department of Homeland Security that enforces immigration laws, conducted hundreds of raids aimed at cracking down on undocumented workers and the people who employ them. Thousands of people were deported.

An estimated two-thirds of the children of undocumented immigrants are U.S. citizens—they were born in the United States. If their parents are deported, the children go with them, and these children usually must leave familiar surroundings and start over in a country they may not know and perhaps have never even seen before.

Debating Immigration Reform

In 1982, the U.S. Supreme Court ruled that all school-age children in the United States are entitled to attend school,

Patients wait for care at a California hospital. Some people have expressed concern that undocumented immigrants place a strain on hospitals and other public services.

regardless of their immigration status. However, many U.S. citizens resent paying taxes to support people who are in the United States without documentation. In 1994, California voters approved a ballot measure known as Proposition 187. The measure, which sought to deny undocumented immigrants the right to education and medical care, was struck down by a federal court. However, the state's many Mexican immigrants got the message that they were less than welcome.

People on both sides of the debate agree the immigration system needs to be reformed. They disagree on how best to go about it, however. Some people favor a law enforcement solution for undocumented immigration. They believe the answer lies in such actions by the federal government as a further tightening of border security, tougher enforcement of laws prohibiting employers from hiring undocumented workers, and tougher enforcement of laws permitting deportation of anyone living in the United States without the required documentation.

Others see a law-enforcement-only solution as unworkable. They would like to bring undocumented workers out of the shadows, especially because many areas of the U.S. economy—particularly agriculture, construction, and the service sector—depend on immigrant labor. To meet U.S. labor needs, some elected officials have recommended creating a temporary worker program. This would provide a system under which immigrants could come to the United States with U.S government authorization to work for a limited period of time.

Advocates of tougher border control want more surveillance cameras along the border, like this one near Laredo, Texas.

Meanwhile, elected officials and others continue to grapple with the question of what to do with the estimated 12 million undocumented immigrants from all over the world who currently live in the United States. Most lawmakers admit that it would be difficult if not impossible to deport them all. Some suggest that many longtime residents should be given a path to citizenship. The Immigration Reform and Control Act of 1986 granted legal status to certain undocumented immigrants—particularly agricultural workers—who had lived in the United States since 1982. Similar proposals put forward more recently would grant amnesty to various groups of undocumented workers, allowing them to apply for legal status. Opponents of these plans say they reward lawbreakers and would only encourage more undocumented workers to come to the United States.

A journalist anchors the morning news at the Univision Spanish-language station in Los Angeles.

CHAPTER FIVE

CHANGING THE AMERICAN CULTURE

In September 1968, Congress authorized National Hispanic Heritage Week to honor the histories, cultures, and contributions of Americans who came from or whose ancestors came from Spain, Mexico, Spanish-heritage countries in the Caribbean, and Central and South America. The annual seven-day celebration was to begin on September 15, the date in 1821 when five Latin American countries—Costa Rica, El Salvador, Guatemala, Honduras, and Nicaragua—declared their independence from Spain. (Mexico declared its independence on September 16, 1810, and Chile on September 18, 1810.) In 1988, the celebration was expanded to cover a monthlong period, from September 15 to October 15.

Yet in many ways, there is no reason to single out one month a year. Hispanic culture is a vibrant part of the patchwork quilt that makes the United States what it is today. The signs are everywhere, literally, in Spanish and English. Traditional Mexican dishes, such as tacos and quesadillas, have become American family favorites. Millions of Americans of all backgrounds enjoy Mexican restaurants. Cinco de Mayo (Spanish for May 5)—a Mexican holiday commemorating the May 5, 1862, victory of Mexican forces over a French army in the Battle of Puebla—has been adopted in the United States in a way similar to the Irish holiday of St. Patrick's Day. Mexican-American culture is a vital part of daily life in the United States. At the same time, Mexican Americans have shaped U.S. culture from the earliest days of the nation.

Ride 'em Cowboy!

Few things are more representative of American culture than the cowboy. Tough, self-sufficient, skilled with a lasso and a gun, the cowboy is a symbol of American independence and strength. Yet the first cowboys were Mexicans. The word *cowboy* comes from the Spanish name for working cattle drivers, *vaqueros* (literally translated as "cowmen").

Kendall Nelson, a photographer and author of the book *Gathering Remnants: A Tribute to the Working Cowboy*, estimates that in the late 1800s about a third of all cowboys in the American West were Mexican vaqueros. Most vaqueros were *mestizos*—Mexicans of mixed American Indian and

Vaqueros brand a steer in this illustration from the nineteenth century.

European heritage. The vaqueros were rounding up longhorn cattle in New Mexico when it was old Mexico and in Texas long before it became the Lone Star State. The border between the United States and Mexico shifted, but the vaqueros continued to work on the ranchland.

"All of the skills, traditions, and ways of working with cattle are very much rooted in the Mexican vaquero," Nelson said in a 2003 interview with the magazine *National Geographic News*. "If you are a cowboy in the U.S. today, you have developed what you know from the vaquero."

Countering Early Stereotypes

Although the first cowboys were Mexican, in early films cowboys were portrayed as European Americans. In those movies, Mexicans were generally depicted as, at best, romantic señoritas (young women) or, at worst, bandits. In the 1960s, Mexican Americans began fighting stereotypes by creating their own cultural identity as Chicanos.

A Chicano artist's mural decorates a highway underpass in San Diego, California.

Politics and the struggle for equal rights were at the heart of much of the artwork, poetry, and films they produced. In California beginning in the 1960s, self-described Chicano artists created posters for the United Farm Workers, the labor union that has many Mexican-American members. Chicano writers such as journalist Ruben Salazar (1928–1970) drew attention to the Chicano political movement and exposed police brutality against Mexican Americans. Poet and political activist Rodolfo "Corky" Gonzales (1928–2005) convened the first Chicano youth conference in 1969. It was attended by many Chicano activists and artists.

Women were a big part of the Chicano activist movement, including labor leader and civil rights activist Dolores Huerta, who along with Cesar Chavez was one of the founders of the UFW. Chicana activists such as Anna Nieto Gomez also challenged the traditionally male-dominated Mexican culture. (Chicana is the term for Chicano women.) In 1971, a group of Chicana activists including Gomez began publishing a Chicana newspaper, called *Hijas de*

Cuauhtemoc, to speak out against sexism. Like other women in the feminist movement that developed during the 1960s and 1970s, Chicanas wanted equal rights and the same chance to pursue work and educational opportunities as men had.

An Epic Identity Crisis

"Yo Soy Joaquín" ("I Am Joaquín") is Rodolfo Gonzales's famous epic poem about Mexicans descended from Aztec warriors and Spanish conquistadors. In the poem, Gonzales writes of the hopes of immigrants, poor but proud, and the discrimination they face. He also explores the cultural differences between Mexicans and Americans. And throughout, he addresses the identity crisis faced by Mexican Americans, who are torn between two worlds and often find a home in neither. Here's how the poem begins:

> Yo soy Joaquín,
> perdido en un mundo de confusión:
> I am Joaquín, lost in a world of confusion,
> caught up in the whirl of a gringo society,
> confused by the rules, scorned by attitudes,
> suppressed by manipulation, and destroyed
> by modern society.
> My fathers have lost the economic battle
> and won the struggle of cultural survival.
> And now! I must choose. . . .

Exploring Cultural Identity

Many current Mexican-American writers continue to embrace the term Chicano. One such writer, Gary Soto, was born in Fresno, California, in 1952. He writes poems, novels, and short stories for children and young adults set in California's Mexican-American community. His books are written in English, but they often include Spanish words that he defines in a glossary. Like many Chicano writers before him, Soto is also active in his community. As the young people's ambassador for the United Farm Workers and for California Rural Legal Assistance, an organization that seeks to ensure that low-income rural areas in California have access to legal services, he often visits schools to talk about these organizations.

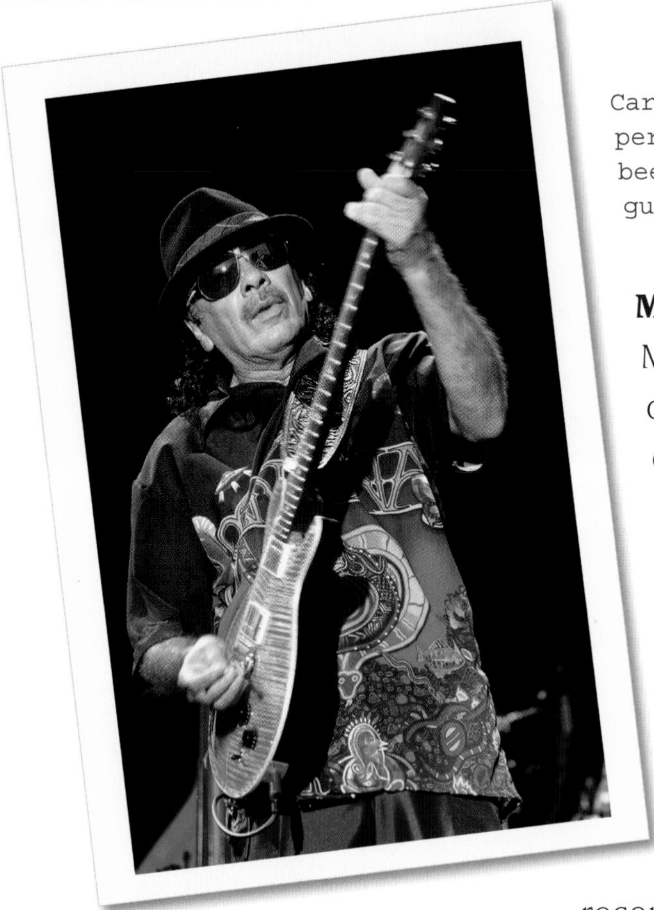

Carlos Santana, shown here performing on tour in 2008, has been called one of the greatest guitarists of all time.

Music and Politics

Mexican-American music is often political. Many of the earliest Mexican border ballads were protest songs that railed against injustice. In the 1960s and 1970s, folksinger, musician, and composer Joan Baez (b. 1941), who is of Mexican and Scottish descent, was one of many performers who recorded hit songs about social issues. Baez also was an outspoken supporter of civil rights and was active in the anti–Vietnam War protest movement during the 1960s and 1970s.

Pop singer-songwriter Linda Ronstadt (b. 1946), whose father was Mexican American, began her career in the mid-1960s as a folksinger and went on to win awards for music performed in a variety of styles. Mexican-American rock and roll pioneer Ritchie Valens (1941–1959) had his biggest hit with a rock version of the Mexican folk song "La Bamba" in 1958, shortly before he was killed in an airplane crash. The song would be a hit again in 1987, when the Mexican-American band Los Lobos recorded it.

Spanglish

Mexican Americans often talk to each other in "Spanglish," a mixture of Spanish and English. Spanglish speakers commonly toss in phrases from both languages—sometimes in the same sentence.

This **duality** is the basis of the 2004 film *Spanglish*, which explores issues of cultural identity. The movie features the Mexican-American actor Shelbie Bruce as a teenager who moves to the United States from Mexico with her mother. The mother, who speaks little English, finds work as a maid in Los Angeles. She relies on her daughter to translate for her. The daughter is quick to embrace American culture. While the mother wants her daughter to succeed, at the same time, she wants her to be proud of her Mexican heritage. Straddling two cultures, the daughter struggles before she finds her own identity as a Mexican American.

Shelbie Bruce *(right)* with actor Paz Vega, who plays her mother, in *Spanglish*.

One of the best known Mexican-American musicians today is Carlos Santana (b. 1947). He first came on the music scene in the 1970s with his band, Santana, which blended rock, blues, salsa, and jazz fusion. More than thirty years later, he was still recording hits. In 2003, *Rolling Stone* magazine listed him as one of the greatest guitar players of all time.

Media Savvy

As the Mexican immigrant population has increased in the United States, so have the sources of news and entertainment in Spanish. In 1990, there were 355 Spanish-language newspapers in the United States. By 2008, there were almost 550. The number of Spanish-language magazines doubled between 1990 and 2008, rising from 177 to 352. Spanish-language radio is also big business. Most cities have at least one radio station that broadcasts in Spanish.

Spanish-language television networks are among the fastest growing in the United States. In 2008, Nielsen Media Research reported that Spanish-language news programs attracted more viewers in New York City and Los Angeles than comparable news shows broadcast in English. This growth is "a clear indication of how the U.S. is changing," Ray Rodríguez, president of Univision, the leading Spanish-language media company in the United States, told the *Associated Press* in August 2008. Researchers at Hispanic Business Inc. estimate that by 2010 advertisers will spend $4.3 billion trying to reach the growing Hispanic market.

Ready for Prime Time

From 2002 to 2007, Mexican-American comedian George Lopez produced, wrote, and starred in his own television series on ABC. The show, called *George Lopez*, was a comedy about a Mexican-American family living in Los Angeles. Much of it was inspired by Lopez's early life.

"I always felt invisible, and I was louder in my own head than I was verbally," Lopez said in an interview with the *Los Angeles Times*. "I was torturing myself, wanting to say things and not knowing how to. . . . So to have something that's named after me make it . . . it's unbelievable to me because I never really thought anything good would happen to me."

Henry Cejudo rejoices after winning a gold medal in wrestling at the 2008 Summer Olympics.

A Fighting Chance

Wrestler Henry Cejudo fought hard to make his dream—winning an Olympic gold medal—come true. His mother, Nelly Rico, taught him that anything was possible if he worked hard. Nelly Rico crossed the border from Mexico at age fifteen with little more than high hopes. When Cejudo was four, his mother, who worked two jobs, moved him and his five brothers and sisters from South Central Los Angeles to Phoenix, Arizona. Cejudo was a star wrestler in high school in Phoenix. At the 2008 Olympics in Beijing, China, Cejudo, at twenty-one, became the youngest U.S. freestyle wrestler to win a gold medal.

The list of Mexican-American boxers is a long and notable one. One of the most successful, Oscar De La Hoya, was born in East Los Angeles in 1973. Reporters nicknamed him "Golden Boy" after he won a gold medal in boxing at the Barcelona Summer Olympics in 1992. In 1996, he beat his own idol, Mexican boxer Julio Cesar Chávez, for the World Boxing Council super lightweight title. Through early 2009, De La Hoya had won thirty-nine of forty-five professional matches.

More than 150 Mexican Americans were among the 350 people who became U.S. citizens at a swearing in ceremony in Phoenix on July 4, 2007.

CHAPTER SIX

LOOKING TO THE FUTURE

The history of Mexican Americans in parts of the United States predates the current national boundary. In states such as Texas and California, Mexican Americans have not forgotten that they were there first. Still, in spite of their long history in the United States, or perhaps because of it, many Mexican Americans tend to live apart from the wider U.S. community and feel they have few friends outside their own culture. Many live in predominantly Mexican-American neighborhoods where Spanish is more widely spoken than English.

These often historically Mexican-American areas grew in size as many new immigrants arrived in recent decades. The neighborhoods offered a safe haven from discrimination and a support system for newcomers, especially those who did not speak English or who lacked documentation.

Mexican-American Officeholders

In 2009, Hilda Solis, who had been a member of the House of Representatives from California, became President Barack Obama's secretary of labor. Solis is the daughter of a Mexican-American father and a Nicaraguan mother. Other Mexican Americans have also made their mark on American government. Mexican American Henry Cisneros became the first Hispanic to lead a large U.S. city when he was elected mayor of San Antonio, Texas, in 1981. In 1993, he joined President Bill Clinton's **cabinet** as secretary of housing and urban development. Cisneros was the first Hispanic to hold that position.

Other Mexican Americans who have served in prominent government positions include Romana Acosta Bañuelos, who was appointed U.S. treasurer by President Richard Nixon in 1971, and Lauro F. Cavazos, who served as secretary of education from 1988 to 1990, during the presidencies of Ronald Reagan and George H. W. Bush. Federico Peña, who had become the first Hispanic mayor of Denver, Colorado, in 1983, was U.S. secretary of transportation from 1993 to 1997 and U.S. secretary of energy from 1997 to 1998, during Bill Clinton's presidency. Alberto Gonzales, the grandson of Mexican immigrants, served as U.S. attorney general from 2005 to 2007 under President George W. Bush.

President Obama speaking at a press conference where he introduced Hilda Solis *(far left)* and other new members of his administration.

However, these same neighborhoods have also kept many Mexican Americans segregated from the wider American community. That, in turn, has limited their ability to acquire the English language skills they may need to find better jobs. Poorly performing schools in many of these neighborhoods have often failed to help later generations move on.

The United States has historically expected immigrants to assimilate. To be American means learning English and adopting U.S. values. Mexican Americans who live in regions with large Mexican-American populations may feel less need to integrate with the wider American society, however. A study reported in the 2008 book *Generations of Exclusion: Mexican Americans, Assimilation, and Race*, by Edward E. Telles and Vilma Ortiz, found that only 17 percent of second-generation Mexican Americans (those whose grandparents had come to the United States) had married non-Hispanics. Even after three generations, the study found, descendants of Mexican immigrants still are likely to identify themselves as Mexican American rather than simply American. On the positive side, the researchers found this tendency to be an expression of pride in Mexican Americans' cultural identity. On the negative side, however, they also found it often stemmed from a sense of separateness born of generations of discrimination by the wider American community.

A Move Toward Citizenship

In 2006, only 21 percent of the foreign-born Mexican-American population eligible for citizenship had chosen to become U.S. citizens. That's half the rate of all immigrants eligible for citizenship. (Immigrants are allowed to apply for citizenship after they have been permanent legal residents for five years. Those who are married to U.S. citizens may apply after three years of permanent legal residence.) That trend, however, seems to be changing.

In 2007, 122,000 Mexican-American immigrants became U.S. citizens, a 50 percent increase over the previous year. A number of factors contributed to this sudden jump.

Mexican Americans and other Hispanics voted in record numbers in the 2008 presidential election, sometimes waiting in long lines, such as this one in Phoenix, to cast their ballots.

Government actions pointing to a crackdown on undocumented immigrants was one of them—even documented immigrants wanted to guarantee their status by becoming citizens. The Spanish-language media also launched a massive campaign urging people to apply for citizenship in advance of the 2008 presidential election. As citizens, Mexican Americans have voting rights—and that could prompt big changes in U.S. policies toward Mexican immigrants.

"Immigrants are tired of the tone and tenor of the immigration debate, which they feel is humiliating and does not recognize their contributions," said Rosalind Gold of the National Association of Latino Elected and Appointed Officials' Educational Fund in Los Angeles in an interview with the *Los Angeles Times*. "That climate has fueled their desire to have their voices heard."

Growing Political Clout

For a long time, Hispanics barely tapped their potential political power. According to the U.S. Census Bureau, only 7.6 million Hispanics voted in the 2004 presidential election—slightly less than half of all eligible Hispanic voters. Less than a third voted in the 2002 and 2006 congressional elections. Yet Hispanics represent a large—and growing—group of potential voters. Even according to conservative estimates, by the year 2020 at least 12 percent of eligible American voters will be Hispanic. Based on an analysis of Census figures, the Brookings Institution, a nonprofit research organization, predicted that by 2020 nearly a quarter of eligible voters under thirty will be Hispanic.

Young Mexican Americans are becoming more politically active. In 2006, tens of thousands of Hispanic students joined nationwide protests against what they saw as unfair treatment of immigrants, including proposed legislation that would make it a **felony** to be an undocumented immigrant. That bill did not pass, but its introduction drew loud protests from Mexican-American immigrants and their children. Waving handmade banners that read "We're not criminals," "We are the future," and "We are the American Dream," they marched in cities across the United States. "We've been here for many years. We work hard. We contribute to the economy of the United States," eighteen-year-old Fermin Vasquez, a student from Los Angeles, told a reporter for the *Associated Press*.

Immigration reform was one of the issues debated in the 2008 presidential election campaign. Early in the campaign, New Mexico Governor Bill Richardson became the first Hispanic to seek the Democratic nomination for president of the United States. Although Richardson ended his candidacy in early 2008, several months before Barack Obama secured the nomination, Richardson's presence in several **primary** elections may have inspired many Mexican Americans and other Hispanics to register to vote.

On Election Day in November 2008, Hispanic voters turned out in historically high numbers. Major news organizations estimated that some 10 million Hispanics voted—more than a 30 percent increase over 2004. News organizations also estimated that about two-thirds of Hispanic voters cast their ballots for Barack Obama, who

Antonio Villaraigosa *(right)*, the first Mexican-American mayor of Los Angeles in more than a century, greets Mexican President Felipe Calderón *(center left)* during a 2008 visit by Calderón to Los Angeles.

became the first African American elected president of the United States. Hispanic votes may have helped Obama win several states with growing Hispanic populations that had been won by Republican George W. Bush in 2004.

As a U.S. senator and in the campaign, Obama favored a U.S. immigration policy that included stronger border controls, improvements in the immigration process to make it easier for people to come to the United States as documented immigrants, and providing a path to citizenship for undocumented immigrants who are already in the United States.

City of Angels

In 2005, Antonio Villaraigosa, the son of a Mexican immigrant father and a California-born woman of Mexican descent, won a hard-fought battle to become mayor of Los Angeles, making him the first Hispanic mayor of the City of Angels since 1872. Los Angeles, the nation's second-largest city and the U.S. city with the highest population of Mexican Americans, represents some of the best and worst aspects of life for Mexican Americans. The city takes great pride in its Mexican roots and is home to many thriving businesses owned by Mexican Americans. Yet many of the newest immigrants have few job skills and stand on street corners hoping to pick up work as day laborers.

Villaraigosa knows both sides of life as a Mexican American. He grew up in East Los Angeles, a poor area troubled by failing schools and violent street gangs. Villaraigosa was expelled from a Roman Catholic high school for getting into a fight after a football game, but he later graduated from a public high school and earned a bachelor's degree in history from the University of California, Los Angeles.

"I will never forget where I came from," Villaraigosa told supporters after becoming mayor of Los Angeles. "And I will always believe in the people of Los Angeles." Villaraigosa's success offers hope to Mexican Americans that the American dream is within their grasp.

FACTS ABOUT MEXICAN AMERICANS

Characteristic	Mexican Americans	Percentage for Mexican Americans	Total U.S. Population	Percentage for U.S. Population
Total population	28,339,354		299,398,485	
Male	15,019,858	53%	146,705,258	49%
Female	13,319,496	47%	152,693,227	51%
Median age (years)	26		36	
Under 5 years old	3,400,722	12%	20,957,894	7%
18 years and over	18,053,339	64%	224,548,864	75%
65 years and over	1,191,614	4%	35,927,818	12%
Average family size	4		3	
Number of households	7,115,059		111,617,402	
Owner-occupied housing units	3,628,680	51%	74,783,659	67%
Renter-occupied housing units	3,486,379	49%	36,833,743	33%
People age 25 and over with high school diploma or higher	7,881,174	54%	164,729,046	84%
People age 25 and over with bachelor's degree or higher	1,167,581	8%	52,948,622	27%
Foreign born	11,391,556	40%	37,547,789	13%
Number of people who speak a language other than English at home (population 5 years and older)	19,768,683	79%	55,807,878	20%
Median family income	$37,940		$58,526	
Per capita income	$13,140		$25,267	
Individuals living below the poverty level	6,518,051	23%	38,921,803	13%

Source: U.S. Bureau of the Census, 2006 American Community Survey estimates

GLOSSARY

amnesty: Pardoning or overlooking an action that violates the law; for example, amnesty for undocumented immigrants allows them to continue living in the United States without facing any legal penalties.

annexation: Adding new territory to an existing country.

boycott: A form of protest in which people stop buying a particular product or using a particular service.

cabinet: A group of people who advise the president on important issues.

coyotes: The name for smugglers who bring undocumented immigrants into the United States.

culture: The beliefs, customs, and way of life of a group of people.

deport: To remove a person or group of people from a country.

discrimination: Treating people unfairly because of race, age, religion, ethnic group, or other reasons.

documented: Referring to immigrants who have official government documents, such as visas, that give them permission to live, study, or work in the United States permanently or for a period of time.

duality: Being made up of two different or opposing things.

economy: The way a country makes and uses its money, natural resources, goods, and services.

felony: A serious crime for which the punishment is often severe.

green card: The informal name for the identity card that proves an immigrant has U.S. government authorization to be a permanent resident of the United States.

Hispanic: A Spanish-speaking person of Latin American or Spanish descent.

immigrant: A person who travels to another country, usually to settle there.

immigration: The act of traveling to and entering a new country, usually to settle there.

missionaries: People who teach and spread their religion, usually in foreign countries.

prejudice: Negative judgments about a person or a group based on such things as race, religion, ethnic group, or economic status.

primary: An election held by a political party to pick that party's candidate to run for office.

repatriation: Returning people to their country of origin.

sentiment: A feeling, attitude, or opinion.

stereotypes: Commonly held, often negative, ideas about the characteristics of an entire group of people. Stereotypes do not take into consideration the individual differences among people belonging to any group.

subsidy: Money given by the government to help businesses or individuals; for example, subsidies given to farmers help them make a profit from growing and selling their crops.

surveillance: Close observation of a person, group, or area, often conducted by law enforcement officers.

tariffs: Taxes imposed on goods that are imported or exported.

undocumented: Referring to immigrants who enter and remain in the United States without obtaining the permission and paperwork required by U.S. law.

visa: A document that indicates a person has permission to enter the United States and to remain either permanently or for a certain period of time.

TO FIND OUT MORE

Further Reading

Alegre, Cesar. *Extraordinary Hispanic Americans*. New York: Scholastic, 2006.

Cruz, Bárbara C. *Triumphs and Struggles for Latino Civil Rights*. Berkeley Heights, NJ: Enslow Publishers, 2008.

Davis, Barbara J. *The National Grape Boycott: A Victory for Farmworkers*. Mankato, MN: Compass Point Books, 2008.

Ingram, Scott. *Mexican Americans*. Milwaukee, WI: World Almanac Library, 2007.

Perl, Lila. *Immigration: This Land Is Whose Land?* New York: Marshall Cavendish Benchmark, 2009.

Perl, Lila. *North across the Border: The Story of Mexican Americans*. New York: Marshall Cavendish Benchmark, 2002.

Senker, Cath. *The Debate About Immigration*. New York: Rosen Publishing, 2008.

Websites

http://memory.loc.gov/learn/features/immig/mexican.html
This section of the Library of Congress website includes a history of Mexican Americans in the United States, with links to learn more about different aspects of that history.

http://southwestcrossroads.org/index.php
This interactive site on the culture and history of the Southwest includes primary source texts, poems, fiction, maps, paintings, photographs, oral histories, and films that allow users to learn more about people in the region.

http://www.pbs.org/kpbs/theborder/history/interactive-timeline.html
This site contains an interactive timeline of the history of Mexico, the Southwest, and the changing U.S.-Mexican border.

BIBLIOGRAPHY

The author found these sources especially helpful when researching this volume:

Batalova, Jeanne. *Mexican Immigrants in the United States*. Migration Policy Institute, April 2008: http://www.migrationinformation.org/USfocus/display.cfm?id = 679

Dear, Michael. *Monuments, Manifest Destiny, and Mexico, Part 2*. The National Archives, Summer 2005: http://www.archives.gov/publications/prologue/2005/summer/mexico-2.html

Passel, Jeffrey. *Mexican Immigration to the US: The Latest Estimates*. Migration Policy Institute, March 2004: http://www.migrationinformation.org/Feature/display.cfm?ID = 208

Ramos, Jorge. *The Latino Wave: How Hispanics Will Elect the Next American President*. New York: HarperCollins, 2004.

Telles, Edward E., and Vilma Ortiz. *Generations of Exclusion: Mexican Americans, Assimilation, and Race*. New York: Russell Sage Foundation, 2008.

Notes:

Chapter 2:

Page 16: "I must say as to what I have seen of Texas . . . " Davy Crockett letter published at www.thealamo.org/Crockett%20Letter.htm

Page 20: "Ballad of an Immigrant." http://southwestcrossroads.org/search.php?query = keyword%3A + Immigration + and + Naturalization + Service

Page 23: "Here in Ventura County, we're trying to . . . " http://www.loc.gov/ammem/afctshtml/tshome.html

Page 24: "In the farms we would do anything . . . " http://www.farmworkers.org/testmony.html

Page 29: "Dear Mr. Wallace . . . " http://www.pbs.org/wgbh/amex/zoot/eng_filmmore/ps_youth.html

Chapter 3:

Page 34: "I was born in Mexico, but . . . " Reprinted with permission of The Advocates for Human Rights. http://www.energyofanation.org/41db3975-0ca4-4898-9a4f-c990d328c26c.html?NodeId

Chapter 5:

Page 59: "Yo Soy Joaquín . . . " Reprinted with permission from the publisher of "Message to Aztlan" by Rodolfo "Corky" Gonzales (© 2001 Arte Público Press, University of Houston)

All websites were accessible as March 21, 2009.

INDEX

Page numbers in **boldface** are illustrations, tables, and charts.

About the Series Consultant

Judith Ann Warner is a Professor of Sociology and Criminal Justice at Texas A&M International University (TAMIU), located in Laredo, Texas, near the U.S.-Mexico border. She has specialized in the study of race and ethnic relations, focusing on new immigrants to the United States and their social incorporation into American society. Professor Warner is the editor of and contributed a number of essays to *Battleground Immigration* (2009), a collection of essays on immigration and related national security issues. Recognition of her work includes the 2007 Distance Educator of the Year Award and the 1991 Scholar of the Year Award at TAMIU.

About the Author

Jayne Keedle was born in England. She spent two years in Mexico City before immigrating to the United States at age sixteen. After graduating from the University of Connecticut with a degree in Latin American Studies, she worked as a newspaper journalist and then as an editor for *Weekly Reader* classroom magazines. She lives in Connecticut with husband, Jim, and stepdaughter, Alma. As a freelance writer and editor, she has written a number of books for young adults. Her books in the New Americans series are her first for Marshall Cavendish Benchmark.